Fighting Th

Copyright © 2022 Jahzeal Clarke
ISBN: 9798357611420
Published by NspireMe2B Publications LLC

Birmingham, Alabama

www.nspiredauthor.com.com

Contents

Acknowledgments

It is with great gratitude and appreciation, that I would like to acknowledge and thank God for His love and care for me. I'm thankful that He has set me apart; equipped me with the willpower, strength, and inspiration for such a time, as this. He has enabled me to write this book using my experiences for His glory and impact other lives out there so that faith might be gained in exchange for fear and stretched - so that trust can be multiplied in a trustworthy God.

I would like to thank my (betrothed) fiancé, Danaia Roberts, for her prayers, support, and continued encouragement. Acknowledgment and thanks to everyone on the journey, who has encouraged and continue to encourage me along this path, and that has encouraged me to put my story in a book.

Acknowledgment to my late mother, Ms. Audrey Henry, who transitioned back in 2004, while I was at the tender age of 10 years old. Apart from her moral support, my mother worked very passionately to financially support the family. She is my main influence: she has taught us to love and care and the morals of life, as a result, I'm humbled and appreciate the lessons taught to us, including the work ethics, by my beloved mother.

Special thanks to my neighbor, Ms. Joyce Watts, who has been very kind and thoughtful to me and at times played the role of a mother in some sense. Ms. Watts had given me my first Christmas present, she would give me a few dollars when I was in need - she would even correct my grammar when I would speak and my sentences didn't make standard, English sense.

Acknowledgment to, Megan Duncan, for being on the team, to assist me with the writing and editing of my book. Acknowledgment to my publisher, NspireMe2B Publications, for having done a good job publishing my book.

Introduction

As we sojourn through this life, we're all affected by challenges at one point or another – only, each of us has different measures of the challenges we experienced. However, some never rise above their challenges because of a lack of faith. Moreover, it's not necessarily that their challenges were unbearable, but because they lacked the faith in God that gives one hope, to endure. This is not to say that the challenges that some of us are faced with are not extremely difficult, but the word of God clearly states that He will not give us more than we can bear. **1 Corinthians 10:13 KJV** *"There hath no temptation taken you, but such as is common to man: but God is faithful, who will not suffer you to be tempted above that ye are able; but will with the temptation also make a way to escape, that ye may be able to bear it."* One cannot serve God without faith, as there will be times when one will pray and don't see a result in one's prayer, immediately – because the answer might be ye' no or wait - but will need to have faith that God hears one's prayer and will answer – in one form or another. **Hebrews 11:6 KJV** *"But without faith, it is impossible to please him: for he that cometh to God must believe that he is, and that he is a rewarder of them that diligently seek him".*

Nevertheless, God is willing to sustain and keep those who lacked faith, from being drowned by their circumstances – if they only believe. Most of the time when we're betrayed, physically, spiritually, or physically hurt, it's usually by someone close to us. Like Cain of the book of Genesis, who murdered his brother because of jealousy, every family has that one member who is plagued with the same spirit as Cain. The spirit of jealousy is very dangerous, it will try at all costs to stop your dream – worst-case scenario, it could murder you to kill your dream.

Genesis 4:1-9 KJV *1 "And Adam knew Eve his wife; and she conceived, and bare Cain, and said, I have gotten a man from the LORD. 2 And she again bares his brother Abel. And Abel was a keeper of sheep, but Cain was a* *tiller of the ground. 3 And in process of time it came to pass, that Cain brought of the fruit of the ground an offering unto the LORD. 4 And Abel, he also brought of the firstlings of his flock and of the fat thereof. And the LORD had respect unto Abel and to his offering: 5 But unto Cain and to his offering he had not respect. And Cain was very wroth, and his countenance fell. 6 And the LORD said unto Cain, why art thou wroth? and why is thy countenance fallen? 7 If thou doest well, shalt thou not be accepted? and if thou doest not well, sin lieth at the door. And unto thee shall be his desire, and thou shalt rule over him.8 And Cain talked with Abel his brother: and it came to pass, when they were in the field, that Cain rose up against Abel his brother, and slew him. 9 And the LORD said unto Cain, Where is Abel thy brother? And he said, I know not: Am I my brother's keeper"?*

After the death of my mother, I, too, have had my faith tested, my life shaken, by the hardship, that as a child, and a teenager, have challenged me. This occurred at the most troublesome times in my life when I least expected them. I've had family members casting spells on me as a child and teenager, trying to destroy my life. I've had days when I was hungry, lonely, and had no one to love and care for me. Nevertheless, God had a plan for my life, but He was about to turn these circumstances around for my good, the devil meant for bad! Moreover, God was preparing me for the same physical; a spiritual, and mental battle that I was faced with and have had to endure – those experiences have equipped me with the spiritual qualities and abilities needed.

My humble beginning

1 Timothy 6:12 KJV *"Fight the good fight of faith, lay hold on eternal life, whereunto thou art also called, and hast professed a good profession before many witnesses"*.

I grew up in a working-class family and lost my mother at the age of ten years old, but these humble beginnings and the tough upbringing moulded me into the wise past student leader and the servant of God, that I am today. I was born and bred on the island of Jamaica (in the constituency of eastern St. Andrew) Kingston Jamaica, Papine Mona commons area, across from the University Hospital. Therefore, I was raised in those areas from birth to ten years old when my mother fell ill, and her illness deteriorated and took a turn for the worse.

Therefore, she passed away at Mona Heights, where we lived! I was considered the youngest of all my siblings because I was very close to her – I even inherit some of her traits such as selflessness, help, and care for others. I am the sixth of ten children that were born to my mother. I primarily had just my mother around who worked very hard to ensure that we were fed and schooled. My father was not around but I can recall having a stepfather at one point. My mother was a vendor who sold various items to make a living and to financially support the family. At the time, I attended Mona Heights Primary School, but I had challenges with reading as I could not read well, and neither did I have the support of my mother as she was either too busy or wasn't able to read herself to assist me.

Nevertheless, the pivotal time for me began when I entered grade (year) four: I realized that everyone in the class could read but at a different level. There was this darkness and gloominess that I felt, but I had a desire to experience the joys of being able to read, and a determination to learn. Therefore, I was determined to push myself - with the little faith I had, and the Lord helped me.

There was a reading class and there was this teacher who took an interest in me and taught me to read. Later, as I progressed to a higher grade such as grade six, I was given GSAT Exam but failed it as I had no understanding of what was written on the exam paper as it was very complex and challenging.

During this period, my mother passed away and this impacted me severely: I was traumatized by her death and was shattered by the fact – which played a vital role in my failure in my early childhood education. Two years after the death of my mother, and during this period of attending Primary School, the family was visited by some Police Officers whom my aunt tried to convince, to take my siblings and I, (an institution for children) to what we would call a 'Boys Home' in Jamaica. However, I remember hearing the officers saying that we were bright children who have too much potential, to be placed in a home.

Everything was going very bad and neither there was no sign of improvement in sight. As a result of all these experiences I have had during all those spiritual experiences and trying times, my relationship with God has been very, purposeful. Nonetheless, I continued to align my steps to following God's path and will, for my life. Nevertheless, God has created divine interventions for me to get external assistance from people who have shown selflessness towards - me with the school being a major part of my assistance, including alumni.

Also, some people have been significant in contributing to the development of my life. Nevertheless, I was further transferred and placed at New Day Primary and Junior High School located at Dulwich Road, Barbican, in Kingston Jamaica – that was the turning point for me.

At this point, I began to experience and know who God is; The Lord began to empower me as I cried out to Jesus about the loss of my mother and everything I was going through and the fact that I had no one to support and care for us. At one point the principal wanted to transfer me to a different school because I was not living up to the standard of the school: most times I was late because I didn't have food to eat – but things were about to change. Nonetheless, I thank God for my neighbor Ms. Watts, who took interest in me and the time and saw it fitting to prepare porridge sandwiches for me to take with me to school for my lunch. And because I've always been kind and caring, I use to find pleasure in sharing my sandwiches with my classmates: and if it were thirty students that were in the classroom, all thirty of them would have had a chance to take part in sharing my sandwich with me – at some point or another. However, even though I was being provided breakfast, whenever possible, by Miss Watts (who was a tremendous help to us), my neighbour, at times after school I came home and there would be no dinner to eat.

Therefore, I would resort to mangoes - morning, noon, and night - to satisfy my hunger. At times, when I couldn't see in the darkness of the night, I would just close my eyes and feel around for a mango on the tree. It was then decided to find a job as a cleaner, to clean dogs' feces from people's homes. After school, I would walk around and ask people whether they need my assistance to clean up their dogs' feces from their yards for a small change. Nonetheless, I began to clean their dog's feces up and I would earn myself a JMD 200.00, 150.00 (JMD) Jamaican Dollars, the equivalent of 0.99 cents (USD) US Dollars or 0.83 (GBP) Great Britain Pounds. Sometimes I would earn JMD 200.00 which is equivalent to $1.32 (USD) US Dollars and £1.11 (GBP) Great Britain Pounds. This is what I would use to help the dull situation such as my past hunger state, and I would use the money to back a bag of juice and a bun, to satisfy the hunger and to make it through the day.

My household foe

I can recall back from 2013 to 2014, I was at my highest level of achievement, and looks like I was beating the odds and breaking generational curses. However, things were about to take a turn for the worse. I began to experience a spiritual blow coming from my maternal side of my family members, which was being hurled at me. I recall having just one pair of school uniforms (khaki pants and a white shirt) that would wash each evening at the end of the school day so I can have a clean uniform to wear to school the following morning.

Moreover, there was a particular morning I went outside to retrieve the pants that I hung on the line the previous night after washing, therefore, I began to iron my uniform to wear to school that morning. I begin to smell Olive Oil, and to my surprise, when I looked, there were several patches of oil stains on my pants, on different sections - "but how is this possible when I have washed them, the previous night"?! I thought to myself. It is due to my relationship with God, I was able to identify things that are occurring in the spirit realm. I could always decern whenever there were spirits near, had I not developed a relationship with God over the years, I would not be able to decern occurrences.

Moreover, although I was young, I had a relationship with God, therefore, He graced me with the ability to decern that something wasn't right. Nonetheless, I then took my pants to my grandmother and bring her attention to the oil stains, "Grandma, look at these oil stains on my pants", however, she ignored me and advised me to wash my pants, but I didn't as it wouldn't make sense to wash it as I had washed it the previous night.

Moreover, I went ahead and prayed, and got dressed for school, wearing the same pants. Nevertheless, I got dressed and headed to school that morning, but an unimaginable happened: while walking, I felt a mighty and compelling force pulling my feet into the busy road! I was being involuntarily pulled in the direction of moving vehicles, against my will! Nevertheless, I began to pray in the name of Jesus and the dark spiritual force got subdued! This is one of those instances where the word of God came to life – as He is faithful to His word! **Psalm 91:11-12 KJV** *"For He shall give His angels charge over you, to keep you in all your ways. In their hands, they shall bear you up, lest you dash your foot against a stone."* I know This might sound a bit weird to some, but I decerned that the spiritual blow was coming from one of my (aunt) mother's sisters, with the intent to destroy me. Nevertheless, Jesus had forewarned us and has written in the book of **Matthew 10:36** *"And a man's foes shall be they of his own household."*

So that one may have a better understanding of me and the reason I had become unwell at a very early age. As previously stated, my mother had ten children and I am the sixth child. As a young boy, I was very clingy to my mother, therefore, I was believed by many, to be the tenth child because of my clinginess. Moreover, I believe the Lord has blessed me with visions, the ability to see, to understand certain things, and the ability to create. Therefore, I've always wanted to be there for my siblings and to be the one to make a change in our circumstances – by setting the pace so that everyone else could follow suit. I was identified as the one who was going to make a difference among my siblings and change our circumstances - hence the spiritual attack that was impacting me physically, as I was targeted from within.

My progression

After Junior High School and New Day Primary where I wrote the grade nine achievement test and pass, I was one of the top students. Therefore, I earned myself a place at the great St. Andrew Technical High School and matriculated as a new student – with the help of God - which was a life-changing experience for me! There was a time in my life when I didn't believe in myself or my self-worth until I heard about Jesus and had a desire to search for Him and know Him for myself. Ever since I met Him, my self-esteem has become heightened, and it has been fulfilling and rewarding to serve Him. As a result, I have become a better person than I was before I had any knowledge, of Him, and I am still growing and improving each day. I am now walking in me and better understanding my purpose. Every aspect of my life began to re-developed, my mind and who I was as an individual. The Lord was working through me, helping me to know myself and my worth. **Mathew 10:31 KJV** *"Fear ye not, therefore, ye are of more value than many sparrows"*.

Moreover, I went back into ninth grade and tenth grade and became the head boy and was doing exceptionally well in the business class and progressed to graduating from the sixth form at St. Andrew High School with nine CXCs and six Capes, and eventually matriculated to the university - which made me the first of the ten children of my mother to progress to university. I recall at times when I would attempt to study at night, my aunt would switch the lights off to prevent me from studying and stated that for me to freely used the light to study, I would first need to pay the light bill - mind you, I was just a high school student who did not have a nine to five job, provide food for myself - let alone pay the light bill.

Nevertheless, I decided to resort to studying under the streetlight there were times when I would even fall asleep right there under the lights. Following this, one night I thought to myself, the university campus is there, and I normally usually see people studying under the Gazebo studying. I was so keen to learn that, on one occasion I jump over the fence of the (UWI) University of the West Indies, Kingston, but was caught by security. The university gate is normally opened on some nights, but for some reason, it was closed that night. Therefore, I decided that I was going to jump over the fence with my backpack of books and study all night for my exam. Moreover, being that I was wearing a type of clothing that blended in - which made me appear to be one of the students - except that I did not have an ID card. Only to my surprise, when I entered the university compound, I saw a light shining from around the corner - which I thought was just a car but only to find, it was one of the University Police. He asked whether I was a student and I replied yes, I am a student - as if I was a student at the University but I lied. Moreover, I was threatened with detention by the guard - because according to him, what I did was a serious offense.

Therefore, I was transported to a security office, in his car where I apologized for lying to him. Moreover, when I began to explain to the guard, the reason for my action (that I needed somewhere to study), he was touched with compassion and agreed for me to go on the campus to study, but only asked that whenever I'm going there that I should first make him aware, and they will look out for me as it's illegal to being there at a certain time and not being a student there. After a while, the security guard and I became good friends, and I maintain a connection with the security officer as he follows my progress and is very pleased with me.

Unfortunately, during my time in high school, I became homeless. One evening, upon returning home from school, I was greeted with a newly changed lock on the door. My aunt had changed the door lock, and ever since then, I no longer had access, to the home. That was the home I lived in as a child with my mother, but I was evicted by my aunt - as my mother was no longer around. Therefore, I resorted to an old, abandoned building where I slept on the hard, cold concrete, for nights, weeks, and months - and made it my home – as I had no-where else to call home. Whilst sleeping in the old, abandoned build-ing, I had a sense of loneliness and feeling of being unsupported by my family and others alike. Sleeping rough had given me a sense of humility and a different perspective on life that no matter one's state of living, life can change at any given time, and place us in a spot we didn't bargain for. Life can sometimes hit you from any direction. Furthermore, it was a situation I had to resort to, just to survive for a time. Even though I had to resort there, I didn't feel hopeless as if it was the end, I just felt like that was me going through a particular storm and God was with me. Here I am, sleeping inside an old, aban-doned building, having to silently make my way through, because I had to enter someone's gate to get to the back of the yard where the abandoned building was – that I had discovered was a spot that I could rest my head from the cold and the rain, the dew of the night, and the cold, somewhere that I could get a night's rest. Nights after nights, whilst discreetly making my way to (the old, abandoned build-ing) my temporary home, I could hardly see in the dark, so I had to use my phone's flashlight to see, as I made my way through the neigh-bor's home to get to the building. Moreover, when I entered the building and was ready to rest my head for the night, wherever I laid my head it remained, and wherever I placed my feet that's where they remained for the night, as I laid there, unbalanced and in an awkward position, but at least I had a roof over my head. Somehow, somewhere deep on my inside, I didn't feel as though that was it for me as if that's the best that life had to offer.

Even though I was there in that condition, I was still praying, and God was there with me. Yes, I was rejected and felt abandoned, but I was always encouraged, and God has taught me through my struggle, and I have always received strength through things that have come to break me down or to pull me back. That has always been over the years what I used to ignite a flame within me more by the grace of God, therefore, that was there, which I just had to endure that storm for that time, and I got greater strength, meaning, and purpose to push me forward. There was a time that I used to attend school so of course, I used the experience to work a little harder, to think a little straighter, to fight a little more, so that at the end of the day I could be and make a difference so that my words are more clearer when I encourage people and teach the gospel of the kingdom, precise and fierce and so that my stance in life is better and I had a greater purpose in me, so I used the situation to stand stronger and better, as an individual.

Nonetheless, there was a lady that took me in when I was homeless, she stressed to me that all the hardship I had gone through was enough for me to be a notorious gunman. Instead, I went to school, educated, positioned myself, and became a role model and an example to my peers. Although I could have chosen the wrong path by taking up guns – as other young men do, I have never been easily influenced negatively because I had my own beliefs and who makes my own choice. Moreover, I have always chosen to be different and kept to myself, as I considered myself to be a leader. However, there was one occasion when I decided to go along with a friend in school to one of the classrooms of the younger students, but little did I know that he was up to no good. Moreover, we went to the class not knowing he had an intention of stealing a student's phone. The following morning, she was taken to our classroom to identify us – which she did, and we were both suspended for a few days. Ever since that, my name has never been mentioned in such action and I had become the head boy and progressed.

Wrongly profiled and stigmatized

James 1:1-4 KJV *"My brethren, count it all joy when ye fall into divers temptations; Knowing this, that the trying of your faith worketh patience. But let patience have her perfect work, that ye may be perfect and entire, wanting nothing".*

On one occasion, I was visiting one of my aunties but there was one night that I couldn't sleep well: as I lay there in the dark inside my cousin's room, I felt a sense of loneliness as my aunt was not at home that night. Therefore, I decided to sleep in a particular section of the house – the front, to be precise. Strangely enough, in the middle of the night, the television switched off by itself and I wondered how was that possible when I didn't personally switch it off.

Therefore, I thought why I should switch the television back on since I wasn't the one who switch it off, but whilst in my cousin's room that night, I felt the urge to urinate, so I reached over in the dark and to my surprise, I felt an object and realize that it was a bottle. Therefore, began to use it as a bedpan - as I was afraid to go outside the other section of the house, to urinate. I began to urinate when the unimaginable happened. I noticed that the texture of my manhood suddenly changed: it felt like the texture of a play-doh in my and felt as if the skin was falling off! I quickly reached for my bible and began to read *Psalm 91*; my cousin overheard me and switched the lights.

Also, everyone else heard me reading the bible and woke up. Whilst reading the bible, a hole appeared inside it, but I continued reading until the hole disappeared. I then decided to leave the house, just to get away from my so-called family and all the atrocities that were happening, there.

Nevertheless, it was about midnight, but the doors and gate were open, so I left – even without wearing shoes on my feet. I was ada mant about not staying there but had nowhere to go, I just wanted to get away from there and as far as I possibly, can.

Therefore, I headed down the road to the Mona Heights area, and I saw a car coming down the road towards me and I kept walking, but little did I know that it was a Police vehicle. The closer the vehicle come toward me, the clearer it had become that it was a Police car. Therefore, they got out of the car and came toward me, standing by the Police was my aunt who was trying to convince the Police that (I did not have full, mental capacity) something was mentally wrong with me.

Unfortunately, the Police were convinced and believed my aunt's word as she was the adult, and I was the child. I was not given the chance to explain to the officers that I was mentally sane and that nothing was mentally wrong with my brain. Eventually, I was taken into the Police vehicle and taken to the University Hospital and was tied up and injected in both my feet. What was injected into my feet, I do not know, but I recall praying and asking God to cause my system to excrete whatever I was being injected with. While I was still praying, the supernatural happened: I could taste chemical as it was being excreted, through my mouth! During that moment, all I could hear was my aunt telling the medical professionals that "*Something is wrong with his head*"! The first foot was injected but when the second foot was being injected, I lost concentration, therefore, not all the chemical that was injected in the second foot was excreted, as I was a bit distracted and lost concentration. This was a very harsh treatment by my family, labelling me mentally ill to the point where I was tied to a bed and injected despite all the other traumatic experiences I have had – including the death of my mother at such a young age.

The Lord came to my rescue

One day at school, I recalled how I lost focus and became absent-minded. I was in school one day when I was awarded 'head' boy in STATHS, sixth form: I was there collecting my badge but couldn't, and neither did I hear when my name was called - I just wasn't connected. Moreover, I began to feel people pulling me toward the Podium to collect my achievement, but no one seem to be aware of what was happening to me. After leaving school that evening, I headed to Maxfield Road Spanish Town, where St. Anne's Technical High School is located, to conduct a transaction.

Moreover, I felt an excruciating pain deep within the cavity of my chest: I could feel a hole in the top left of my chest that was getting wider! I quickly got a taxi and headed toward the Halfway Tree area, in Kingston. I've always been the type of person who can withstand pain: hence I was able to get a taxi to continue my journey back – despite the pin I was experiencing. Moreover, I arrived at Halfway Tree, and as I crossed a road and made my way towards the Bus Park, whilst walking with my head hung in pain. Around the park were people asking whether I was ok. There was a lady who was concerned with my appearance – as I was still in pain and it was obvious, that I was. "Young man, are, you ok", she asked, "Yes, I am" I replied – as I had always had a way about me that no matter how excruciating the pain I am feeling, or how unhappy I was anyone asked whether I'm ok, I would always wear a mask of being ok when I was not.

Nonetheless, the lady continued to communicate with me and insisted that I was not ok. Using her initiative, she flagged down a taxi and took me to the Andrews Memorial Hospital. Moreover, my condition worsens and grew daunting; and as I sat there in a wheelchair waiting to be seen by a doctor, with dangling limbs and a head that was falling backward, things were about to drastically change, for the better!

This is the moment where I was going to be graced with the opportunity to see Jesus and to be in His presence – in a lifeless state! Although my body had become lifeless, I had to wait to be seen as the staff was trying to retrieve my record to register me – so that I might be seen. During this time, a teacher of mine, Mr. Lawrence, who was my mentor and still is, from (STATHS) St Andrew Technical High School, visited me and provided information regarding needed for my registration. While I waited, limped, and powerless in the wheelchair, with a loss of control of my hands and feet, I knew that I was going through spiritual warfare, as I was still alert – regardless of my loss of mobility. Nevertheless, I prayed, *"Lord, you can't just take me like this, I want to be here to look after my siblings and to impact people's lives. Please give me a chance to get well and live and represent you, if you give me a chance it will be me living for you, my time of living for me will be over"*! Immediately after praying that prayer, and whilst my eyes were still closed, I saw a bright light and I knew there and then, that it was Jesus Himself! He came to me at the lowest times in my life, when I was experiencing the (witchcraft) blows of the spells that were cast for my life by those who should have loved and cared for me.

Moreover, I was eventually registered and was taken to a ward where I was admitted. Although powerless and limped, I can recall being subsequently placed in bed, curtains being drawn, and the doctors attempting to prescribe medication and make a diagnosis for a spiritual problem with a physical solution. Again, the curtain was drawn, and as I lay there by myself, then I remembered what the songwriter said, *"There's power in the name of Jesus"*, and I began to call on the name of Jesus. I called on the name of Jesus! Instantaneously, felt like whatever I was going through (the pain, the hole, and the void) in my system, were being repaired!

Nonetheless, I continued calling on the name of Jesus Christ again and that made the difference, there and then. I didn't want to be overheard and stigmatized by the doctors as being mentally ill, therefore, I tried not to speak too loudly but discreetly called on his name again and went deeper. And as I continued to call on the name of Jesus, I began to experience a shifting; instantly my eyes begin to open, and I thought to myself, *"This thing is real"*! I called Jesus again and the hole that I previously felt, deep inside the cavity of my chest, began to decrease in size until it was closed, and my strength begins to restore, then I begin to realize that something supernatural was happening within my life, and my body! As the mighty shifting and re-vamping were taking place in my hospital room, I began to experience for the first time in my life, that the name of Jesus was not just any other name that I was calling on but there is power attached, to that name! The name of Jesus drives away demons; it heals the hole and fills the void, it makes demons nervous and hell tremble, it interrupts the enemy, restores your soul, and gives you everlasting peace. Fur-thermore, I could have laid there suffering in bed and it would have taken the doctors nothing to misdiagnose me as having a natural ill-ness, but thanks to God that I knew Jesus, thanks to God that I called on the name of Jesus! I could have called on my beloved, angel moth-er but I know that she would not have been able to hear and heal me. I experienced the power of God that came through for me there and then, and this happened at a time when no one understood my pre-sent state, at the time, or touched the pain and let it vanish.

There is 'Power in the name of Jesus' according to the songwriter, and I experienced that for myself. Nonetheless, all the downfall, rejection, illness, sadness, and agony that I have experienced, were predestined for this divine, intervention. This is the Lord's doing and it's marvel-lous because all things work together for good to those who love the Lod, according to the scriptures. **Romans 8:28 KJV** *"And we know that all things work together for good to them that love God, to them who are the called according to his purpose"*.

Previously to this incident, I was doing the things of the world, living a worldly life, and walking contrary to the word of God. At one point I used to drink, party, and wear earrings and locks. However, getting to know Jesus Christ was life-changing for me - as my life's situation brought me to know God. He came to me based on the incidents that life had presented, before me. Hallelujah!! **Jeremiah 33:3 King KJV** *"Call unto me, and I will answer thee, and show thee great and mighty things, which thou knowest not".*

My unwavering faith

Hebrew 11: KJV "*But without faith, it is impossible to please him: for he that cometh to God must believe that he is and that he is a rewarder of them that diligently seek him*". As time goes by, I faltered on my walk with God: I didn't walk away from Him together, but I met and formed a friendship with a lady and became very close. We later conceived and have two children together – a son and a daughter. It so happened that my son fell ill at just four months old. He was having difficulty breathing and we realize he wasn't breathing, properly. Therefore, we rushed him to the Children's Hospital, Kingston, where we had been for four days. The doctor examined my son, and an X-ray was done, but we were told that he had water in his lungs and that a huge percentage of his lungs was taken over by Pneumonia.

Therefore, the doctors decided to admit him for assessment and observation. It so happened that the health professionals began to withdraw blood from his spine. Even though I had dreadlocks and wore tight pants, and still doing things contrary to the words of God, I still attended church. Therefore, my faith would not allow me to accept those words of discouragement. However, hearing those hurtful words coming from the doctor regarding my son's health; seeing the rising death toll of other children, night after night - that would be transferred by staff over to the nearby Morgue, during the night, and hearing the cries of the parents in the morning got me so concerned but my faith did not waver.

Nevertheless, I decided not to leave the hospital until my son gets looked after by a doctor and discharged. As a father, I was committed to remaining with my son at the hospital because I did not appreciate how some of the staff mistreated children at the (Bustamante Children's Hospital) hospital, at the time - and currently. As a result of being at the hospital for weeks, all the resources and money I had we used up by us. Therefore, I remained at the hospital for days without a shower – but occasionally I would change shifts with the mother of my children so that I could go home and have a shower. Moreover, one night whilst the lead doctor was running the ward and updating parents on their children's health, the doctor came over to us and stated that my child might not make it. Having been told by the doctor that my son had only a fifty percent chance of living, and it was highly likely that he would not make it, my faith kicked, and I knew that God would heal him. that was the green light for me to decide to commit my life to God. **Romans 8:8 KJV** "*And we know that all things work together for good to them that love God, to them who are the called according to his purpose*". Moreover, I prayed, and I heard the voice of God saying that I will have to make a sacrifice to Him so that He can make a sacrifice for my son's healing despite the doctor's report. The sacrifice I was required to make was to recommit my life to God and make Him first place, and I did just that. Nonetheless, I made the sacrifice to God; I went down into the Water Grave, got baptized, having heard the baptism song "*The water is troubled my friend, step right in God almighty power is moving this hour*" being sung, and recommitted my life to God! Having done all of this, my son miraculously recovered and healed.

Unfortunately, whereas children were dying and being transported to the Morgue – which was located on the premises, and amid seeing parents weeping and wailing for their deceased children, I was able to leave the hospital with my son! The process was a lengthy one, but I am ever so thankful to God for healing my son, taking us through this and my son is bubbly, up and running. I will never cease to praise God for all that He has done for me!! There is nothing too hard for God – as stated in the book of Genesis. **Genesis 18:14** *KJV* "*Is anything too hard for the Lord? At the time appointed I will return unto thee, according to the time of life, and Sarah shall have a son*".

From misery to Ministry

Having experienced homelessness, hunger, nakedness, and all the challenges, I feel strongly that God has allowed me to encounter these things to prepare me for my current, ministries. Had I not experienced these hardships and difficult situations, I would not have felt the need to reach out to the homeless, naked, and hungry. Basically, as a ready pen in a writer's hand, I made myself available to do service for God by clothing the naked, feeding the hungry and where possible, housing the homeless. To raise awareness of person's stories about their medical stories who require medical assistance, I use my platform to accomplish such. For example, for persons that are not financially unstable and require medical assistance, or have needy situations, I used my platform to highlight their situations to solicit help for them with whatever financial aid I can, personally contribute.

Also, I publicly preached the gospel of Jesus Christ and minister to persons through prayer and words of encouragement, directing them to God and several of these individuals have been saved through the ministry. Also, I travel from Parish to Parish, locally and internationally from church to church, train to train, streets to streets, to highways and byways, preaching the good news of the Kingdom of God. In addition to that, we evangelize overall through the ministry, over the years, through the support of Jamaicans locally and abroad, we're able to assist homeless single mothers and fathers with children by building homes for them and caring for the holistic development of people: physically, socially, spiritually, and mentally alike.

Furthermore, my ministry speaks for itself in terms of how it all started and how it gave birth to me starting Jamaica's first-ever Food Bank. As a result, I was inspired and started my apparel business called 'Christ Royalty Apparel' where I am in the business of selling shirts, hats, and anything that has Christ's divine signature statement on them. I am humbled to say, my work such as community development and leadership has been recognized by the government, and the Queen of England. I have seen people's lives transformed, people turn to Jesus, and souls being saved. Also, I have been able to see my ministry materialize, houses are being constructed and hundreds of people are being fed through the ministry. Ever since I began to attend Primary school, and have been involved in different clubs and societies, I have dedicated myself to 'service above self'. Service above self is about serving beyond self, not for selfish reasons or personal motives, by literally going beyond the call of duty putting my pleasures and needs aside, just to assist others to make a difference. Nonetheless, as I travel abroad to preach the gospel of the kingdom to others, I can see God's hands blessing and providing. He made provisions in terms of Airfare, travel, clothing, and shelter, among many other things. He also made a way for my children by providing for their needs. Nevertheless, I will never cease to trust Him not to abandon my faith as a city of prayer!

Moreover, I do not seek success or to be awarded by man, but one thing I know is that whatever I aimed to do, I have always been able to accomplish and impact the lives of others. **Mathew 25:35-40 KJV** "For I was an hungered, and ye gave me meat: I was thirsty, and ye gave me drink: I was a stranger, and ye took me in: 36 Naked and ye clothed me: I was sick, and ye visited me: I was in prison, and ye came unto me. 37 Then shall the righteous answer him, saying, Lord, when saw we thee an hungered, and fed thee? or thirsty, and gave thee drink? 38 When saw we thee a stranger, and took thee in? or naked, and clothed thee? 39 Or when saw we thee sick, or in prison, and came unto thee? 40 And the King shall answer and say unto them, Verily I say unto you, In as much as ye have done it unto one of the least of these my brethren, ye have done it unto me".

From nothingness to success

Nonetheless, I matriculated to the (UWI) University of the West Indies - which happened to be the compound of very university that I had made an unauthorized entry, to study under a Gazebo and was Apprehended and almost penalize. Moreover, I have completed my five years of studies, and have achieved my qualifications. Nevertheless, I thank God for His love, His grace and mercy!!! What the devil meant for bad, God has turned around for my good.

Although life has been challenging for me growing up, I have made most of these accomplishments through very astonishing circumstances such as studying under a streetlight, going without proper living necessities, most of the time and sleeping on cold concrete. I'm certainly not new to everyday challenges, and neither am I inexperienced in fighting nor rising above life's obstacles. I was described by my past teachers as being 'relentlessly, helpful and determined. I have developed an interest in Governance, Politics, Leadership, Nation Building, Youth Development, Economics, Sports, and Social Development – which taught him that there's nothing greater than to offer oneself, for service.

By God's grace, I was able to tailor my skills to meet the needs of various learning situations. I have become one of Jamaica's most promising youth leaders. Today, I am a gifted leader with over ten years of experience working in social justice and political activism. I have learned the streets' philosophies of St. Andrew, Jamaica – which I have combined with a thirst for learning. As previously stated, I was the first in his family to have graduated (from St. Andrew Technical High School) at the top of my class: my excellent grades have won me admission to the University of the West Indies. My academic skills made history and I was recognized by the Queen of England for my work/achievements. Over the years, I have served simultaneously as 'National Spokesperson and Youth Mayor of the prestigious National Secondary Student's Council movement. I have also served in leadership positions as 'Class Monitor, Student Council President, Vice President, Past Deputy Head-Boy, Past Deputy Youth Mayor for Kingston & St. Andrew, Current Youth Mayor for Kingston & St. Andrew, Prefect, and Head-Boy. Also, I served as Region1's first Vice President for the National Secondary Student Council (NSSC) and National Spokesperson for the United Nations Youth participant, Kingston & St. Andrew Youth Advisory Council Member, J.C.F/I.S.S. A Peace for Champs Campaign. Also, I was recently appointed one of Jamaica's (JP) Justice of the Peace.

Also, recently, I was selected to be part of the Aspire-ers society and the Royal Commonwealth. Therefore, God is always there in terms of success!

Jeremiah 17:7-8 KJV *"Blessed is the man that trusteth in the Lord, and whose hope the Lord is. For he shall be as a tree planted by the waters, and that spreadeth out her roots by the river, and shall not see when heat cometh, but her leaf shall be green; and shall not be careful in the year of drought, neither shall cease from yielding fruit".*

Final thought

I would like to say that my story matters, and I need to have shared it with the world. Often, people believed that their stories do not matter, but I would like to say how important my story is to me and for the world to read it. Oftentimes people tell their stories to others, it means nothing but to those who hear, my story is of immense importance to me, and it was good that I had to endure the hardship so that I can share it with my children, my family, and the entire, world. People need to know and understand the various obstacles or challenges that they may have had to endure - be it physical, spiritual, or emotional, that is not the end of it all.

We have not just over-loaded by that which we face, but through faith in God, and the divine purpose that is in our lives. When our purpose is connected to us, and purpose will bring us out and beyond what may have dictated to us, we will be crippled, and we will die in our situation and not move forward. It is the divine purpose that will get us on the other side of our belief.

May my story be an encouragement to all who have read it because I was inspired by God to share it with the world. I pray it will reach many, changed lives, and win souls. No matter what you're going through, believe in God, have faith in Him, and know that with Him all things are possible. According to the scripture in the book of Hebrews, **Hebrews 11:1 KJV** *Now faith is the substance of things hoped for, the evidence of things not seen.* There were times when I couldn't see but I believed, by faith, that God was there with me and that He can pull me through *'the Valley of the shadow of death, like the Psalmist, King David, states, in the book of* **Psalm 23 KJV** *"The Lord is my Shepard I shall not want. He maketh me to lie down in green pastures: He leadeth me beside the still waters. He restoreth my soul: He leadeth me in the paths of righteousness for his name's sake. Yea, though I walk through the valley of the shadow of death, I will fear no evil: for thou art with me; Thy rod and thy staff they* *comfort me.*

Thou preparest a table before me in the presence of mine enemies: Thou anointest my head with oil; my cup runneth over. Surely goodness and mercy shall follow me all the days of my life: And I will dwell in the house of the LORD forever". I have seen signs and the shadow of death, but I was pushed into a place to connect and topped into the presence of God to give me strength and purpose in all things that I had faced throughout my journey, thus far. My written journey is there as a witness and to let anyone who could use my testimony as an encouragement, know that you're not limited, especially, with the word of God. God has promised to bring us out of whatever circumstance that we're being faced with. It is in reading, that your faith and strength can be harnessed so that you may receive the kind of words and encouragement in the scriptures that can ignite that that place within you that you can be restored to being refreshed, revived, and made whole.

Many people today are experiencing spiritual warfare and have been labeled one way or another. They might even be labeled as being '*mentally ill*' but faith in God through all the chapters in my life and this book has helped to mold and shaped me into the individual that I am today. What I have experienced is a reflection of what thousands of other persons worldwide, have experienced.

I can recall on one occasion, as a young child, I was going through my gate and by the time I stepped outside, I looked up right at the barrel of a gun. But God protected and preserved my life. As I lived in a very violent community, where I have seen men slinging their guns, and having seen the atrocity that my mother had experienced within the family, I could have reverted to gun violence, as other young men have, to avenge my mother.

But unlike other young men my age, I have decided to take up the sword - which Is the word of God, instead of man's sword (the gun). Furthermore, I have had the option of choosing God and I could have never chosen a better way out. I am here telling my story but maybe my story could have been told, but differently – had I not chosen the way of the Lord. Moreover, I am here sharing and inspiring that Jesus is the way out, **John 14:6 KJV** *"Jesus saith unto him, I am the way, the truth, and the life: no man cometh unto the Father, but by me"*.

Having suffered the atrocities at the hands of my aunts who physically and psychologically abused my siblings and I, they have attempted to associate with me after seeing the growth and achievements that God has done in my life. They began to say that I am their nephew, and they are the ones who fostered me. However, I bear them in my prayers and forgive them, but I disassociate myself from them as Jesus has told us to be wise.

Nevertheless, I hold no grudges towards them because of the suffering I endure at their hands, but one thing I know, my journey makes me stronger and wiser! Hallelujah!!!!! **Mathew 10:16 KJV** *"Behold, I send you forth as sheep amid wolves: be ye therefore wise as serpents, and harmless as doves"*. People will hurt you, but do not remain bitter and angry, just pray for them and move on because God will avenge you in due course. As the scripture rightfully states in the book of **1 Thessalonians 4:6 KJV** *"No man goes beyond and defraud his brother in any matter: because that the Lord is the avenger of all such, as we also have forewarned you and testified."* you must remain positive, pray, and hope in God and He will avenge and uplift you in due course. Whatever you do, no matter how difficult the situation, just wait on the Lord. We are encouraged in the living word to wait on the Lord, according to **Isaiah 40:31 KJV** *"But they that wait upon the Lord shall renew their strength; they shall mount up with wings as eagles; they shall run, and not be weary; and they shall walk, and not faint"* I have seen God bless and uplift my siblings and I from the dungeons of life and kept His word that if I seek Him first and His kingdom, all things will be added to me. **Mathew 6:33 KJV** *"But seek ye first the kingdom of God, and his righteousness; and all these things shall be added unto you"*. My siblings are improving and increasing by God's grace.

My sister is doing well in her job, one of my brothers finished his studies at the Art Academy and is currently working in the food catering sector whilst the others are working in various fields to help themselves. I am now in courtship (dating) and will be getting married in the future to my fiancé. Whilst studying at the (UWI) University of the West Indies, in 2019, I met my fiancé, Danaia, while walking on campus. As she seemed discouraged, I began to encourage her by assuring her that everything was going to be ok. At the time, she wasn't in her best mood as she was trying to get some stuff sorted regarding her course, but having challenges, because things weren't going in a particular way as she desired. Therefore, I began to impart the words of God to reassure her that God is in control and that He's in the midst. Therefore, that's how we met, and we continued to have a deep conversation inside the university library. Nevertheless, I continued to encourage her, and we were beginning to get to know each other a little bit.

However, our relationship began to get more serious, but it was on an off-and-on status until we began to converse again – until, in 2021, we decided to take the leap of faith and build on our relationship. When we met, she was not a Christian but eventually, she became a Christian in her church. Nonetheless, we officially decided to build on our relationship and God has ever since been working between us. Danaia has been ever so supportive of me and my ministry: she significantly supports me morally, spiritually, and otherwise. We fast, pray together and study the word together and share the word. Also, she supports my growth, always speaking that life within me and reminding me of my purpose. Furthermore, she has more than a support, she has been a power bank, a tower of strength for me – by the grace of God. Nonetheless, in terms of our future, we planned to 'tie the knot' and get married by the grace and mercy of God by 2023.

Also, we planned to do more work together in the ministry and within whatever ministry, she will be doing too, and with the food bank just serving and trying to live the best life by the grace and mercy of

God. Therefore, that's our future, plan. I do believe that when we come together there's greater that will be achieved as we try to build more in the kingdom of God, continuing to impact lives and reach souls – maybe do a few businesses together, you never know, write a book together or two. I believe there's no limit to what God has for us, you never know what God has for us.

Made in the USA
Middletown, DE
17 October 2022

12606529R00022